SURVIVING NUCLEAR TERRORISM

By Bill Weaver

Copyright 2011 by Bill Weaver

Sheridan Publishing

Bristol, Virginia

ISBN: 978-0-9647960-2-7

Cover design by Endoxos, Deviant Art

Contents

ACKNOWLEDGEMENTS

I am pleased to acknowledge my son Paul and my daughter Shelley for their prompt attention to detail, and repairing my many errors in Microsoft Word 2007. I am also indebted for their uploading the document to Create Space and Kindle. I wish to thank my wife, Margaret for motivation and inspiration along the way.

INTRODUCTION

This primer is essentially the lesson plan I used to instruct U.S. Army Reserve Components in Surviving radiation. Much of the information within was culled from many sources including various U.S. Army Field Manuals, Federal Emergency Management Administration (FEMA) materials, Emergency Management Institute (EMI) study guides, internet sites maintained by The Communicable Disease Center (CDC), Nuclear Regulatory Commission (NRC), Atomic Energy Commission (AEC), and other government sources.

During the recent Fukushima Dai-Ichi nuclear plant disaster, my wife would ask me various questions as the scenario unfolded. I answered every question and then one day she asked "How would I find this information?" I told her to start by reviewing my lesson plan and notes. She said "That's just a jumble of notes in a bag. Why don't you write a book?" I replied "There's no market because the public can research the subject on the internet for free!" In turn, she answered "I'm not just anyone and I don't want to look up all this information available. I just want the salient points in book form and also a copy for each of the children. So, I dusted off my notes and this primer is the result.

Before the first Gulf War, while instructing in Nuclear Warfare, I remarked to my classroom of fellow army reservists, "Radiological Defense is our greatest weakness and consequently, the greatest threat to our security." This was before the rise of the Al-Queda terrorist network and the bombing of the World Trade Center, so the majority of the class, with a few exceptions, viewed me as an alarmist. Until the tsunami struck the nuclear reactor site in Japan they have been right. I still fear the aging one-hundred and four nuclear reactors in our country are a continual danger to all of us.

Listening to the radio during the days of the Cold War the program would often be interrupted with a grim announcement stating, "This is a test of the emergency broadcast system," followed by a shrill high-pitched siren sound of thirty seconds duration and the concluding announcement of "This is a test." Fortunately for us, we never heard the alarming possibility spoken, "This is *not* a test." This book addresses the survivability in such a situation.

Information about nuclear warfare and survivability abound; but for potential survivors in search of a quick reference and needy reminders this primer should add to their store of knowledge.

I hope you never have to use this information.

A Nuclear Explosion

Eyewitness accounts agree the first indication of a nuclear blast is a bright white or yellow flash. Even those persons not facing the explosion notice the intense brightness in the corner of their eye. Peered upon, the flash will cause serious retinal damage and possibly permanent blindness. Survivability begins with your reaction to the flash. The nuclear explosion will release heat and a blast shock wave traveling at hundreds of miles per hour depending on the kiloton (thousands of tons TNT) or megaton (millions of tons TNT) rating of the bomb. Depending on your position and distance to the explosion the effects of the heat and blast could reach you in seconds or minutes.

Estimating range is determined by the arrival of the blast wave or the sound of the explosion and is known as **flash-to-bang time**. This is very similar to the way we measure thunder and lightning where once lightning occurs we begin to count off the seconds to the arrival of the sound. Using one second per mile we calculate lightning being three miles distant if we reach the count of three between seeing the lightning and hearing the thunder. With a nuclear flash the concept is the same except we use a rule of thumb equating five seconds from flash to bang to just over one mile distance (1.1). Consider these examples; the answer is found by thirty seconds divided by our standard of five seconds and then multiplied by the standard of one-point-one (1.1) miles or six times one-point-one equals six-point-six (6.6) miles distance from the explosion. A flash-to-bang time of ten minutes would indicate an approximate range of one-hundred thirty-two miles. (600 seconds divided by 5 seconds=120 times 1.1=132 miles).

Should you be in the open glimpsing the flash and wandering what has just occurred, the heat wave may be upon you before you react, burning or charring all exposed skin tissue. Clothing may protect unexposed skin areas or may burst into flame searing the rest of the body. Should the heat be survived the onrushing blast wave may fling the body through the air like a rag doll slamming into the ground or surrounding buildings with great force for a number of seconds. The greatest danger from the blast wave comes from destruction of structures and the conversion of objects such as rocks, wood, metal, tree limbs, or other objects into missiles that cause striking damage. A victim within the blast radius may become vaporized from the extreme heat produced. A lesser result could produce a human torch roasted into organic material just like strips of burnt meat.

So what is your first line of defense if caught in this perilous situation? First and foremost is 1) get down immediately, preferably behind a solid wall or into a ditch, 2) use your arms to cover and protect your head from blast debris, and 3) remember not to look at the flash keeping in mind the intensity of the illuminating flash may be noticeable through the flesh of your arms while covering your head, 4) wait for the blast wave to pass. Remember this, gamma rays travel at least as fast as the speed of light so no matter what you do the first wave of gamma rays already passed through you.

Once the blast wave has passed your area its possible a reverse wave will return. This becomes possible should the displacement of air in the area of ground zero be sufficient to create a partial vacuum. After the force of the blast diminishes it may return to fill the void left behind albeit at a lesser intensity but still quite sufficient in force in force to cause damage or injury to unsuspecting victims. Remaining in a protected or sheltered area for ten to fifteen minutes after the first blast wave should suffice to allow the reverse wave time to pass. This can be most easily remembered as "watching your backside."

Does taking this action save your life? Is this guaranteed? No way. What it does is increase your chances of survival dependent upon the size and effects of the explosion and your distance and other natural features of the terrain. Proper action may only increase your chance of survival from 0% to 10% or perhaps from 0% all the way to 90%. You will increase but not guarantee your chance of survival.

An individual within an enclosed building upon sensing the first flash glimmer needs to move quickly away from windows as the blast wave shatters the glass into many pieces of shard shredding anyone in its path. An individual moving to a window to explore their curiosity stands a good chance of ending up human ground meat sans the plastic wrap. Add avocado sauce for a sacrifice fit for an Aztec buffet line.

Does it matter what kind of structure provides necessary shelter from the blast? A yield of 20KT breaks all windows within three miles and destroys all wood-frame buildings located within a one and a half mile range. Survival chances are best behind metal, brick, or reinforced concrete. This is easy to remember as "The Three Little Pigs" story where the wolf was able to blow down the straw and wood house but kept at bay and unable to huff and puff and blow down the brick house.

TYPES OF RADIATION

The next problem to consider on the road to survival is the issue of radioactivity. This threat is composed of four types of basic radiation forms: namely; alpha, beta, gamma and neutron. Neutrons are emitted first and directly from a nuclear explosion. Neutrons are extremely dangerous but do not travel far from the blast. Gamma rays generally compose the first radioactive threat to survivors as they penetrate the body easily. Much like x-rays the gamma ray goes straight through a potential victim. However many roentgens the gamma rays are rated will determine an individual actual dose measured in RAD (Radiation Absorbed Dose). Once received the radiation dose is irreversible. Should the dose reach 600 RAD then a lethal dose has been received and death from radiation sickness is probably inevitable. Should the dose received be only 100 RAD this number becomes part of your cumulative dose. The major point here being to avoid gamma rays as much as possible. This can only be accomplished by seeking shelter as soon as the flash is glimpsed.

So, if shelter from gamma rays is necessary for survival, what will protect us? Well, if you were able to dig a hole into the ground and cover yourself with about five feet of dirt then you would have ideal shielding protection. This option is not practical since no one carries around a shovel and besides even if someone did carry around a shovel the time necessary to dig the hole would negate any positive outcome.

Caught in the open the gamma rays will go straight through you much as a sunbather catches the rays of the sun or mimics an x-ray machine. Standing up in the open provides no protection. Should you be in a wood-frame house with no basement you have only slight protection as the gamma rays penetrate with ease. A house in which you can take refuge in the basement provides fair protection perhaps cutting the dose rate in half. Should the house be brick the protection is even better, but the gamma rays are still easily penetrating through the roof. The best protection is a concrete or metal shelter built for this purpose and located in the basement and preferably with three sides covered by dirt.

In all these scenarios you must reach the shelter quickly or the blast wave and heat will cook your future in a matter of seconds. There are a number of manufacturers building radiation specific shelters today, but if you are five miles from home you are not going to make it to a shelter.

Alpha and beta particles are radioactive nuclide byproducts of a nuclear explosion or meltdown and are found in the fallout. Once the blast wave passes the mushroom cloud is rising many miles high into the sky carrying the alpha and beta contaminants with the cloud. There may be a window of opportunity of 20 minutes or 2 hours to escape the area prior to the contaminants becoming fallout and radiating the area for weeks or months to come. Only if you have a radiological survey meter such as a Geiger counter will you know if it safe to move about in any given time frame.

So, once you have survived the neutron and gamma rays the next threat to counter are the alpha and beta particle rays. The alpha rays are the largest in molecular size therefore even the skin acts as a shield. The alpha rays will not penetrate your bare flesh while beta rays do have the capability to enter your body by penetration.

Garments if clothing help to block these agents of contamination. However, they can easily enter through the respiratory system, entering via the nose or mouth, hence the necessary use of a protective mask while in a contaminated area.

POTASSIUM IODIDE

A contaminant such as a radioactive iodine nuclide will be absorbed quite quickly by the body and the material is then transported to the thyroid gland. The thyroid gland just loves the iodine and is the gift that keeps on giving. Radioactivity is absorbed from the contaminant of radioactive iodine until the thyroid enlarges or becomes cancerous.

Children are most susceptible and have a high rate of thyroid cancer when exposed to radioactive iodine unless immediate preventative treatment is instituted. In the midst of nuclear carnage try to remember where you stored the potassium iodide. Finding your medicine cabinet may be the first priority.

The Food and Drug Administration recommends one 130 milligrams tablet within 1 to 3 hours of a radiation emergency. Bull, the government is doing its best but one hour may be too late to save the thyroid gland. Immediate ingestion of potassium iodide (KI) is required to prevent the uptake of radioactive iodine. Do not wait for the government to inform you that it's time to take your pill. Once your thyroid gland begins absorbing radioactive iodine the damage has begun. Swallowing a 130 milligrams potassium iodide tablet one hour late may help to stop further absorption of the radioactive iodine but the odds of thyroid disease remains greatly increased. Important to note is the fact that potassium iodide is only effective against radioactive iodine and only protects the thyroid gland. It provides no protection against the myriad of other radioactive nuclides such as cesium, strontium, tritium, plutonium, neptunium, americium, or curium. There are no other protective agents for these other deadly radioactive nuclides emitted by an explosion and concentrated in fallout.

The potassium iodide preventive dose for each adult is 130 milligrams every twenty-four hours for two days maximum. Infants, children, and pregnant or nursing females are especially at risk.

The Nuclear Regulatory Commission (NRC) recommended dose of KI for an infant up to one month is 16.25 milligrams, one month to three years of age 32.5 milligrams, four to twelve years of age 65 milligrams, twelve to eighteen years of age or up to 154 pounds body weight dose is 65 milligrams. Over age eighteen or 154 pounds the full adult dose is 130 milligrams per day.

Since KI has an unpalatable and salty taste some children may refuse to take the medication. To make the KI palatable, mash the tablet into fine bits and mix with four teaspoons either low fat white milk low fat chocolate milk, orange juice, or a cola. Then administer. Should none of these selections be on hand I can only suggest you try another liquid form. Going to the store through a possible radiation field is certainly not a viable option and besides we know the stores will probably be closed.

Do not ingest KI if you are allergic to shellfish or iodine. Death may result from a severe allergic reaction. So what is the alternative medication you ask? You can kiss your thyroid defense goodbye as there is no known alternative.

For those taking the potassium iodide there are possible side effects that include skin rashes, metallic taste in the mouth, head cold symptoms, diarrhea, swelling of the salivary glands, burning feeling in the mouth or throat, painful teeth, sore gums, and upset stomach. The manufacturers claim side effects usually occur when people take higher doses for a long time. Generally then, side effects are unlikely because of the low dose and the short time you will be taking the drug. The drug is approved for use even if you are taking other medications such as a thyroid hormone or an anti-thyroid drug for a thyroid problem. The FDA recommends you to stop taking the potassium iodide immediately upon the emergence of any of the symptoms and contact your personal health care provider. Hey, good luck with that last piece of advice!

The Nuclear Regulatory Commission (NRC) recommends KI if within a 10 mile zone of radioactivity. Other independent sources recommend KI for up to 200 miles downwind. Personally, I don't think parameters on distance should be used. If you enter or are engulfed by a radioactive or fallout area KI should be taken no matter what the distance.

NRC recommends no more than 48 hours is needed for KI because taking more than the recommended dose may be harmful to the thyroid. The reason offered is the Communicable Disease Center (CDC) says taking too much can cause severe thyroid toxic illness, goiter, or hypothyroidism.

The shelf life of KI is 5 years. Look for the expiration date on the blister pack or other wrapping or container to ensure the KI is current. But, hey, even if the product is outdated, what are you going to do? Best to have a weakened version than none at all if outside it's raining fallout material.

According to the Food and Drug Administration (FDA) potassium iodide is available as an over the counter medication. However, almost every pharmacist I ever asked has replied that a prescription is required. The FDA has removed the requirement for a prescription but many pharmacists are not aware of this fact. I finally had the good fortune to locate a pharmacist that knew KI is a non-prescription medication.

However, he still had to backorder the medication as KI was not part of their everyday stock. Two weeks passed before the medication was available for purchase! The drug is available through online internet sales without a prescription. Why is this so? I can't determine from the answer I received from two separate state boards of pharmacy. Their answer was only intended to sway the public from online purchases and to cast doubt upon online providers as to the veracity of their drugs.

I emailed the following question to both the Virginia and Tennessee Boards of Pharmacy, "I recently attempted to purchase potassium iodide and was informed by more than one pharmacist that I need a prescription. Yet I find the same drug advertised on the internet for sale without a prescription. Please clarify if a prescription is required."

The email reply from the Virginia Board of Pharmacy stated, "I believe the FDA considers potassium iodide to require a prescription. It is important to remember that not all internet sites are legitimate or follow state and federal laws and regulations---."

Probably the best and correct clarifying answer came from the Tennessee Board of Pharmacy, "You may be experiencing a little communication problem. Most pharmacists immediately think of potassium iodide solution or the bulk powder used for compounding the solution which has always required a prescription and was traditionally used to treat thyroid dysfunction and/or some respiratory problems. Since 9/11/2001, various forms of potassium iodide, usually in the form of 130 mg tablets and 65 mg/ml oral solution have been marketed primarily to government agencies for use in treating exposure to radiation. While these products do not require a prescription, they are rarely stocked in pharmacies."

Obviously a supply should be on hand if you intend to prepare for a nuclear explosion. Post explosion not too many doctors will be available to scribble you a prescription, and if they are available, the local pharmacies will probably be permanently closed. Likewise, don't expect the local post office to be delivering the drug even if the carrier can find your mailbox laying in a ditch somewhere. Actually, the federal government in conjunction with the postal service has a plan for this eventuality. The government has prepackaged supplies of KI and the plan calls for rapid delivery by trailer truck to your local post office with further delivery to each and every household in the affected area. More than likely in this example the streets and roads will be littered with corpses of contaminated letter carriers. Do you think the delivery time would fall in the required safety net of one to three hours? Also the local internet service will not connect either. As for your cell phone remember the ad, "Can you hear me now?" because probably no one can. Recent tests, however, indicate text traffic and twittering may be a successful option.

SURVIVAL FACTORS

Surviving in a nuclear radiation zone is determined mainly by three factors; (1) time, (2) distance, (3) and shielding.

Military instructors of nuclear survival are prone to preface their classroom lessons with the following greeting; (1) "Bend over", (2) "Place your head between your knees", (3) "And kiss your ass goodbye." This greeting with heavy mockery attached is used to strongly remind the student that fate may also play a large part in their survival.

Time is important to reduce the cumulative radiation dose received. Distance is important as radiation intensity decreases the further you are from the source as long as the wind is not carrying fallout in your direction or the source is not continuing to emit gamma rays on a regular basis. Shielding weakens or blocks radiation penetration. Best examples of shielding materials are lead, iron, concrete, and water.

Predicting future exposure rates is possible with the **7:10 Rule of Thumb**. This rule is an approximation that states for every 7 fold increase in time after detonation there is a 10 fold decrease in the exposure rate as long as the units remain the same to compare or in this case expressed as roentgens per day (R/day).

Let's put the 7:10 rule of thumb into practice. Assume 24 hours (1 day) after an explosion the measurable exposure rate is 700R/day. Approximate the expected exposure rate in one week hence. The time has increased seven-fold so the expected daily exposure rate would be a ten-fold decrease to 70R/Day.

Using hours as our measurement standard a reading of 100R/Hour after an explosion would have an expected exposure rate 7 hours later of 10R/Hour because a seven-fold increase in time results in a ten-fold decrease in the approximate exposure rate or 100R divided by 10=10R/Hour. Likewise, a reading 14 hours after an explosion would be 100/Hour divided by 10 and again divided by 10 yielding an expected exposure rate of 1R/Hour.

Remember, the 7:10 Rule of Thumb is not precise and only approximates.

If fallout is still descending the 7:10 Rule of Thumb does not apply, as contaminated nuclides will cause the readings to rise.

A radiological survey instrument commonly referred to as a "Geiger counter" is still in use but more modern survey meters have been developed and are now marketed. The layman needs to have available a precise instrument to increase probability of survival.

You may wonder who will tell me what the exposure rate is if I don't have a radiological survey meter. All the local television and radio stations designated will have the latest information garnered by civil defense and public health sources. Tune in to stay updated to the latest changes unless an electromagnetic pulse (EMP) was present from a nuclear detonation. An EMP will damage all electrical components such as televisions, radios, and other communication systems if attached to power lines. Telephones and cell phones may suffer the same EMP damage. We do know a battery-powered radio with a short antenna may survive an EMP and provide your only link to the outside world. Add this item to your list of must-have survival gear.

Also remember, the Russians during the Chernobyl meltdown and now the Japanese with the Fukushima reactors gave misleading or erroneous readings during their crises either from miscommunication, error, or on purpose.

DIRTY BOMBS

Delivery systems for nukes include missiles, artillery shells, depth charges and in the case of terrorism the bombs known as suitcase nukes and backpack bombs.

A suitcase bomb is a portable nuke and is very compact depending upon the nuclide material used in manufacture. The worst case scenario would be 25 pounds of plutonium yielding a 10-20 kiloton explosion. This worst case scenario was dramatized in the Tom Clancy novel *Sum of All*

Fears. Due to continuous technical maintenance requirements this fear is probably way overdone.

A rumor speculates the Soviets designed a portable backpack bomb that can yield a 3-5 kiloton explosion. The rumor has never been substantiated by the Russians or U. S. Department of Defense.

A more likely scenario is a---lone terrorist on a cruise boat circling Manhattan could kill hundreds and perhaps thousands of New Yorkers at lunch time just by lobbing a mortar or two with poison gas or bacteria-germs in them into the crowded streets. "The terrorist could just board the boat with the mortar tube under his coat, set up the mortar on the rear deck in seconds, launch the mortars and throw the tube overboard" the four-star general told me.[1]

A radioactive "dirty bomb" differs from the previous in that it is not a nuclear reaction but a conventional bomb stuffed with radioactive contaminants such as leftover medical or radiopharmaceutical isotopes but most immediate casualties will be blast injuries from the explosion. Once the standard detonation occurs the resultant radioactive material contaminates a wide area necessitating an expensive, dangerous, and time consuming cleanup. But, most importantly, causing wide spread concern and fears among the citizens

---

[1] The Pentagon Labyrinth, George C. Wilson, edited by Winslow T. Wheeler, Center for Defense Information, World Security Institute, Feb. 2011

of the affected nation. A "dirty bomb" is a true weapon to cause panic and terror.

Should you be present in an area affected by a "dirty bomb" you should move inside and as far away as possible to avoid airborne radioactive contaminants. Change your clothes and shoes where possible if you were outside during the detonation to defray the possibility of carrying contamination inside with you. Seal the clothes and shoes in a plastic bag and dispose in a metal container. A shower to wash off contamination may remove as much as 95% of contamination received along with a clean uncontaminated change of shoes and clothing. Listen to the news for further advice.

EXPOSURE VERSUS CONTAMINATION

Here is the difference between exposure and contamination. Radiation is emitted from a radioactive source. You do not have to touch the source to be exposed. When you have a chest x-ray at the local hospital gamma rays penetrate your chest. At that time you are exposed to radiation, but you are not contaminated. There is no residual radioactive material emitting radiation. A radiological survey instrument would not pick up a reading from you. However, you have experienced cell damage from the gamma rays and could become ill or die if the dose is high enough. Now, should you have cobalt inserted into your body for a cancer treatment then you are contaminated. The cobalt is continuously emitting radiation to cause cell damage although the cobalt is medically directed to kill off already cancerous cells. The cobalt also acts as a contaminant. Additionally, you have been exposed to the radioactive cobalt. We won't concern ourselves with cobalt since the material is used for valid medical treatment. What we are most concerned about here is being contaminated by beta particles from a nuclear explosion or accident? A radiological survey meter would begin to "chatter" with a positive reading if passed over a contaminated person. So, in understanding these terms let's remember that a person can be exposed without being contaminated and conversely, a person cannot be contaminated unless exposed.

Now let's consider a controversial and ethical dilemma. Let us assume you are exposed to 400-600 RAD via gamma rays but not been contaminated. Do you go home to or stay with your family or loved ones to be ill and/or die? You can certainly go anywhere you want. You are not a danger to others because there is no residual radiation being emitted from your body even though you have suffered serious cell damage. Conversely, if you were contaminated by fallout or otherwise ingested, inhaled, or absorbed beta particles into your body and are emitting radiation from those particles then should you stay with your family? If you stay with your family while beta or alpha particles, generally from contaminated external skin and/or clothing continue to emit radiation then family members may become exposed due to your contamination. Do you want that to happen? How much radiation do you think they should be allowed to receive? If you are an unexposed and uncontaminated family member are you willing to risk exposure from a contaminated loved one while knowing you may become ill, or face potential life-shortening cell damage, or possibly die prematurely? These are vexing questions. One thing we do know is that without proper survey instruments the radioactive dose emitted from your contamination will not even be known.

The best and only solution to deal with an unknown risk to your family is to complete your external decontamination at a properly designated site. All contaminated clothing is removed followed by a shampoo and body shower. This will help to prevent your family from being contaminated by you. Initially, you may remain contaminated but this should not be a threat to your family. Once you have internal contamination from alpha or beta particles much damage has been done or is being done to your cells. However, some of these particles will be excreted by feces and urine. Consequently, waste products are to be considered contaminated and potentially dangerous.

Another excellent reason to receive decontamination procedures is the site may have a first aid center nearby. The medications administered may help to prevent the further spread of radioactive nuclides in your body. While certainly not near one-hundred percent effective the treatment may perhaps save some lives.

Once death does occur the problem of corpse disposal arises. Should the death occur from exposure no extra precautions need be taken. However, if the death occurred from contaminating radiation certain precautions are required for safety purposes. It is rare for the contamination level to pose problems for burial, but once again we have a situation where a radiological survey instrument is necessary to discern whether radioactivity is present in the body of the deceased. A radiological safety officer needs to be consulted because the element or elements from the incident may have been identified. Some elements such as strontium emit radiation for years and are a public health menace. A worst case scenario must be assumed should the information not be available. The contaminated body should not be burned as the contaminants will be released into the air and possibly contaminate others. The contaminated corpse, in the interests of safety or without other guidance from a radiological official, needs to be buried in a shielding device such as a lead coffin, concrete grave, or much deeper than six-feet to contain any possible radioactivity.

ELEMENTS and RADIATION

Radiation originates in atoms. Atoms are the basis of all matter. The structure of the atom contains a nucleus composed of positively charged protons and neutrons that have no charge. Together the protons and neutrons are collectively named nucleons. Negatively charged electrons orbit the nucleus. The proton and electron opposite charges are equal. Thus, the attraction keeps the electrons in orbit and the atom electrically neutral or stable. These atoms, depending upon the number of protons and electrons have the same chemical properties and are individually called an element. Each is assigned a chemical symbol. There are 92 of these naturally occurring elements.

When an atom differs in the number of neutrons compared to the number of protons the atom is the same element but is referred to as an isotope. Many are radioactive and emit ionizing radiation. Isotopes are also called nuclides and tend to be unstable and the nuclide will attempt to reach stability by injecting energy in the form of radiation. By throwing off particles and energy the nuclides may reach stability as a balanced element. This process is radioactive decay or what we refer to as radioactivity. The ensuing ionization penetrates living tissue and causes a disruption of the cell chemistry.

While there are several types of ionizing radiation, the three most common are; (1) alpha; (2) beta; (3) and gamma. Alpha must get into the body to be a hazard. Likewise with beta although beta can harm skin and other exposed outer tissue. So alpha and beta are mainly an internal hazard. Gamma is pure electromagnetic energy with great penetrating power and is a great external and internal hazard as it disrupts cell chemistry while passing through the body.

HALF-LIFE

The radioactive half-life of a nuclide is the time elapsed for half of the radioactive nuclei to decay. There are huge differences in the rate for different nuclides. Plutonium[239] has a half-life of some 24,000 years. That means whatever reading you measure from plutonium contamination will still be half of today's reading 24,000 years from today! That's why a clean-up would be necessary along with burial in a metal cask and encased in concrete to prevent dire public health risks. Californium[249] has a half-life of 350 years. Iodine[131] has a half-life of eight days so you would think the thyroid would be fairly safe. However, since the half-life is so short that means the iodine[131] is giving off great amounts of energy toward the attempt to stabilize. Hence, the great amount of energy is causing severe chemical damage to the thyroid tissue in a short period of time.

Strontium[90], a beta emitter tends to collect in the bones with a half-life of close to thirty years. Can anyone say "bone cancer?" Plutonium[239], an alpha emitter seeks lung tissue and just one particle may cause lung cancer. While plutonium tends to settle in bones and also the liver, tritium, also a beta emitter, produces genetic mutations and cesium settles into soft tissue.[2]

Strontium is also the culprit that contaminates cow's milk. The cycle begins with strontium fallout settling on vegetation. The cow consumes the vegetation thus causing the strontium to collect in the cow's milk. An unknowing nursing mother drinks the contaminated milk since there is no change in taste or smell to the milk. The milk tastes just dandy to the mother who is now contaminated along with her breast milk. If she breast feeds then the baby will be contaminated with radioactive strontium. Avoid milk in a designated fallout area.

Strangely enough, if we eat the cow we would also be contaminated by cesium attacking soft tissue and also once again we encounter iodine[131] because the nuclide tends to accumulate on vegetation that the cow then consumes. Avoid beef, fish, and other fresh meat along with milk in a designated fallout area. If you have a survey meter available and in you are in a so-called undesignated fallout area and the meter is picking up radiation,

[2] The Silent Intruder, Charles Panati & Michael Hudson, Houghton-Mifflin, Boston, P. 119.

then please consider the area as contaminated. Don't wait for the government to make the decision.

The biological half-life is usually, but not always, less than the normal half-life of a nuclide because the particle is chemically reacting with the cell chemistry of the body to reach stabilization as an element. An example of this reaction is plutonium^{239} with a biological half-life of approximately 100 days versus 24,000 years otherwise. Translation, if you inhale ten nuclides of plutonium^{239} into your body the nuclide will react severely with your lung tissue and will not emit radiation past 100 days although you are dying or have died from untreatable lung cancer. Your corpse may not emit radiation since the plutonium may have stabilized. On the other hand, fallout containing plutonium ^{239} that falls to the ground and finds nothing with which to react will remain only a threat until, carried by the wind or ingested by another animal, finding a suitable material to engage in a reaction. Remember, 24,000 years is the half-life. The remaining plutonium will need another 24,000 years to bring the radiation level to one-quarter of the original amount of emitted radiation level. This is the problem with Chernobyl. The radioactive material contained in the concrete sarcophagus will cause severe heath problems if released. The containment cost over the half-lives is astronomical and the time frame so far out as to be unimaginable.

ANIMAL FOOD SOURCE

Consider all living animals contaminated with radioactivity within a fallout area. Do not eat them unless starvation is the only other option. Should you find no other food source, the alternative is to eat only the animal's muscle tissue. Other parts of the animal such as soft tissue, bone, and organs will contain most of the contaminants. You will have to be careful in skinning the animal and in cutting away the muscle to avoid contaminating the portion you want. Cook the muscle meat well but avoid washing the cut in local stream or river water as it also is probably contaminated. Never, under any circumstance consume an animal that appears to be sick. These directions may not be helpful if you failed biology lab dissection in high school.

Canned meat is the best solution for meat products especially since the containers are generally indoors around a kitchen or storage area that helped to shield the meat items from fallout. Even so, ensure you wipe or clean the can prior to opening. You don't want contaminated particles to fall into the food. Otherwise you will ingest the particles and suffer the consequences. Packaged food will also be safe. Just remember to clean the packaging as you would a can.

Meals-ready-to-eat, or commonly known as MREs, are available on a commercial basis. These are the field rations military members consume. A case of 24 meals is available on line from Long Life Food Depot for about $54. That's pre-fallout price.

Eggs are safe to eat even if laid during fallout.

PLANT FOOD SOURCE

Any vegetable in the garden or fruit on the tree not harvested will be contaminated during fallout. So, the solution is to decontaminate these foods to make them edible and safe. Clean with water if water source is safely available. Vegetables and fruit with a smooth skin are safest to decontaminate with water. Rough skinned edibles should not be prepared this way. The skin should be peeled off the rough edibles and also the smooth edibles as the preferable method of decontamination. Food sources that are underground such as carrots and potatoes are preferable to above ground sources.

Only food already grown can be decontaminated. Planting carrots, for example, in a contaminated garden would yield contaminated carrots as the radioactive particles on and in the ground would be absorbed during the carrots growth stage. Fruit trees also absorb nuclides through their root system that leads to contamination of the leaves and fruit products.

Plants, post radiation, may experience a burst of growth and then turn dark or brown. They get sickly looking as they accumulate radiation.

Eating contaminated vegetables and fruit may irradiate your esophagus, stomach, or intestinal lining. It could cause death. It almost certainly will cause severe vomiting and/or diarrhea, perhaps bloody in nature.

The most preferable food source here is canned food. Canned green beans, baked beans, yams, potatoes, tomatoes, corn, peaches, pears, pineapples, and any other variety you can locate. The can provides a natural barrier against fallout particles and may easily be decontaminated by dusting or rinsing clean prior to opening the can. An added bonus is the liquids in the can. The liquids supplement as a thirst quencher and hydration when contamination of the water supply is likely.

WATER SUPPLY

After a nuclear event, wait forty-eight hours before drinking from an outside source to allow for radioactive decay to occur. Factors such as wind direction, rainfall, and sedimentation will determine whether water has been rendered safe. Underground sources are the safest with water from stream and rivers probably safe after a few days. Lakes and other stagnant sources are likely to be most contaminated.

Use the settling technique to purify water. First, fill a bucket three-fourths full with contaminated water. Then take dirt from a foot or so under the sod and stir into the water. Let settle for at least six hours. The settling dirt will carry the contaminants to the bottom. Dip out the water from the top of the bucket and then filter.[3]

As an additional precaution against disease, treat all water with purification tablets or boil.

The most preferable water supply is one that you prepared in an advance of a nuclear disaster such as stocking your home or shelter with jugs of water. Two to four-and-a-half liters per person per day are required. Another safe source is your own home water pipes before contamination occurs. Fill all bathtubs, sinks, and other available containers with water prior to the arrival of fallout.

RADIATION POISONING

Symptoms of radiation poisoning can include nausea, vomiting, weakness, edema, burns, dizziness, headaches, or red eye due to increased blood pressure. Shock may be exhibited. Other symptoms may occur depending on the tissue or organ most affected.

There is also a condition known as a "nuclear tan." This comes from a 100 RADs or more radioactive dose that causes spasms of the surface

---

[3] U. S. Army Survival Handbook, Lyons Press, 2002, Guilford, Ct, P.337

capillaries in the skin making the face look as if has been powdered.

The weakest part of the body is generally first and most affected by radiation poisoning.

Should you be suffering from emphysema when radiated the first and most serious symptoms will probably be indicative of respiratory distress. That is not to say the bones or pancreas is not affected. It just means the lungs will probably fail first.

Should you be suffering from leukemia the first and most serious symptoms will probably indicate further blood disease. That is not to say other body parts will not be affected. It just means a disease of the blood will probably be the most serious problem to start with. Problems with other body systems will soon follow.

Radiation poisoning is simply a term to indicate the structure of cells have been damaged by a radiation source.

The damage may be acute which is within the first three months such as nausea and vomiting or the damage may be chronic which may occur years later such as cancer. There is a chance your body will heal if the dose was not too high and is received over a longer period of time. This is known as a recovery period.

Some cells are less liable to divide and replace cells such as the brain where a dead cell is not replaced and others divide and regenerate almost continuously such as the intestines.

A British doctor has elicited the following thoughts. These thoughts have not been accepted by everyone to say the least. They include---radiation genetically alters sperm in a way that gives the child a congenital predisposition to leukemia---there will be a totally irrevocable buildup of a pool of recessive genes into the population---never root it out---radiation is the most powerful mutagen known to man.[4]

The Federal Emergency Management Agency (FEMA) agrees to the extent that there will be additional radiation induced genetic disorders across all subsequent generations. Their expectation is based upon animal experiments. Radiation injury to a fetus is a given. Under no circumstance should a pregnant woman be exposed to any level of radiation.

EFFECTS OF RADIATION ABSORBED DOSE (RAD)

This is a general guide. Specific dose rates may affect victims differently.

0-50 RAD. There are no visible effects.

50-200 RAD. There are brief periods of nausea on day of exposure. Up to 50% of survivors may experience radiation sickness with at least nausea and vomiting. Up to 5% may require medical attention. No deaths are expected.

---

[4] The Woman Who Knew Too Much; Alice Stewart and the Secrets of Radiation, Gayle Green, Univ. of Michigan Press, 1999, P. 198, 262, 263.

200-450 RAD. Most members of this group will require medical attention because of serious radiation sickness with symptoms more than just nausea and vomiting. 50% of this group is expected to die within one to three weeks.

600 RAD and above. This is considered the lethal dose threshold. 100% are expected to die following severe radiation sickness.

Again, this is only a general guide. There are other guides that use different ranges. Some may list the lethal dose threshold at 500 RAD while others indicate the body may tolerate up to 100 RAD without visible effects.

A Russian victim in the Ukraine supposedly received a total dose of 140 RAD and within three years the man is all shriveled up, too weak to hold a spoon and has a constant fever of 100.4 degrees.[5] According to our guide he should not be that sick. But then you have the anomalies. Perhaps the radiation attacked his immune system and that may have been his weakest biological area or perhaps the total dose was much higher than reported.

The maximum permissible dose for the civilian population is 0.5 R or roentgens per year (Think of roentgens, REM, and RAD as being equivalent for the time being, although roentgen measures Curies which is the amount of radiation being released into the environment and RAD is

---

[5] Journey To Chernobyl: Encounters in a Radioactive Zone, Glenn Allen Cheney, Academy Chicago, 1995

the radiation absorbed dose while REM is the amount of radiation determined by a formula based upon various particles). That is 500 milliroentgens. This level is set by the World Health Organization to provide safety guidelines around the world. The Environmental Protection Agency (EPA) limits the maximum exposure guideline to 5 REM.

So we can readily discern our main goal is to receive the lowest possible dose. Zero RAD is really what we want because there is **no harmless amount of radiation exposure**.

RAD is still the conventional term used in the United States. The System Internationale (SI) has moved to a metric system. This is the unit used to report on the Fukushima reactors. A RAD is a **Gray (Gy)** under SI. One Gy equals 100 RAD. The U.S. conventional term REM is replaced by the SI unit **Sievert (Sv)**. One Sv equals 100 REM.

PROTECTION FROM RADIATION

Exposure is minimized by time, distance, and shielding.

The less time exposed then the less the dose received. Don't hang around admiring the beautiful mushroom cloud or stop to take photographs of the large plume in the sky. Get out of "Dodge" or "go to ground."

The farther you are away from a source the less intense will be the dose received. However, if you become contaminated, distance will not help, because you will carry the contamination with you. It's only money when they say "you can't take it with you," because radiation will certainly hitch a ride.

Shielding works well to reduce radioactive penetration. The best shielding materials with half-value thickness in order, measured in centimeters, are iron or steel (1.8 cm), brick (5.1cm), concrete (5.6cm), dirt (8.4cm), ice (17.3cm), wood (22.4cm), and snow (51.6cm). The theory of **half-value layer thickness** is exemplified by the fact 1.8cm steel reduces the gamma penetration by half. Then another1.8 cm steel would halve the penetration again. For a total of 3.6cm steel would reduce the penetration another half for a total reduction in gamma level to one-quarter the dose without shielding. So, if the outside gamma radiation read 20R/Hr. or 20 roentgens per hour and you are in a steel building 3.6cm thick then your dose will be approximately 5R/Hr.

In addition to the half-value layer thickness there is the "**tenth-value**" thickness. This means with that barrier the gamma radiation dose will only be $1/10^{th}$ the outside rate. Hence, if the outside rate is 100R/Hr. the inside rate is 10R/Hr. Inches necessary to achieve a "tenth-value" is concrete (11), dirt (16), water (24), and wood (38). So, if you were sheltered in your basement behind an 11-inch thick concrete wall with 16-inches of dirt packing around the wall your effective dose rate inside would be 1R/Hr. Here's how the figures work with an outside rate of 100R/Hr. A basement 11-inch concrete wall cuts the penetrating rate to 10R/Hr. An additional 16-inch of dirt surrounding the basement concrete wall cuts the effective rate to 1R/Hr. Now you can understand why "taking refuge" in a basement is recommended. This simple rule of thumb formula does not take into account any leakage occurring from the upstairs to the basement or leakage from any basement doors leading to the outside.

The prudent defender would barricade the outside doorways and stair entryway with the highest rated material available to avoid contamination via leakage. A minimum two weeks of sheltering is probably necessary.

The problem of human waste must be addressed when sheltering. Going outside into a contaminated area for relief is not a feasible solution as both your and others may become exposed to unnecessary radiation.. Using a corner of the basement leads to a fouling of the sheltering space. Probably the best solution is to plan ahead with the purchase of a portable marine toilet. The cost is about $160. Odor control solution is an extra $20. Cheaperthandirt.com offers a portable toilet for less than $10. The foldable toilet comes complete with legs, rim, and seat along with 6 plastic bags. Additional bags are available for an extra charge. An added purchase of a plastic bucket with lid for about $10 would also be wise to use as a urine collector.

Evacuation and sheltering are the primary methods to avoid radiation. Tune in the local television or radio station for advice on action to be taken and for information relating to the present and future expected radiation dose.

Should you evacuate your home post a sign so family and loved ones know where you are going or can be contacted. The Red Cross maintains a log to reunite families. The telephone number is 1-877-love-is or 1-877-568-3317. You can also access the online log at Red Cross Missing. Cell phones and other telecommunication devices may not work in the affected areas so evacuation to an unaffected area may be necessary before contact can be made. If you make the decision to evacuate please leave before the roads are blocked or travel is prohibited. Homeland Security recommends a list of emergency supplies to keep on hand for a disaster.

The **disaster kit** should include a three-to-five day supply of water (one gallon per person per day), although I recommend two gallon/day/person for two weeks if sheltering, and food that won't spoil. Include a manual can opener. Add one change of clothing and footwear and one sleeping bag per person. A first aid kit that includes your family's prescriptions and medications is necessary. You will need an emergency battery-powered radio and flashlights along with extra batteries. Take with you an extra set of car keys, credit cards, cash, and/or traveler's checks. Take a blank check from your current checking account and see if you can transfer the funds to a new bank should you not be able to return home for an extended period of time. Those of you doing online banking are ahead of the rest of us. You will need sanitation supplies including toilet paper, soap, and plastic trash bags. Make copies of your important family documents and keep with you. I recommend a radiological survey instrument be purchased and kept handy. Firearms are a personal decision. You should try to take as many of these items with you that will fit into your vehicle.

The protective action guides in use by the government plan for a fifty-mile radius evacuation. This is mainly predicated on a radioactive plume escaping from a nuclear power plant. A "dirty bomb" would probably only require an evacuation of a few miles. A fifty-mile radius evacuation will probably also suffice for a low yield nuclear detonation. I recommend you plan for a two-hundred mile radius evacuation. After all, our goal is to accept zero radiation.

Sheltering in your own basement may be an option for you. Hopefully, the basement has been stocked with essential items in preparation for a disaster.

Those of you with big bucks may want to explore the possibility of having your own bomb and fallout shelter built into or adjacent to your home. The major manufacturers are Utah Shelter Systems, Radius Engineering, and American Safe Rooms. All three manufacturers maintain a web page. Remember, if you are not at home when an explosion or accident occurs the shelter may not be of use to you. Also, if your neighbors know you have this shelter expect guests demanding admission. An outside contractor should be used and a satisfactory story concocted if you are asked about any "remodeling."

RADIOLOGICAL SURVEY INSTRUMENTS

You have probably heard this item referred to as a Geiger counter in layman terms. Without this tool you are dependent upon public announcements to inform you of what, where, and how much radiation is present. With your own survey instrument you have the capability to obtain a current reading at any time. Switch on the survey meter for an instantaneous reading should you be on a highway evacuating the area. Should you take refuge in your basement a quick measurement of radiation is available to you. You may find from your readings an extra precaution needs to be taken such as adding more shielding in your basement.

The former civil defense radiological survey instruments on the market today are the models CDV-700 and CDV-715. The CDV-715 is designed to detect high level radiation while the CDV-700 is used to detect low level radiation. Should the CDV-715 not detect radiation that does not mean the absence of low level radiation, only that another survey instrument, such as the CDV-700 is necessary, to measure for the lower ranges. Always use the CDV-715 first as a high level of radiation could jam the CDV-700 rendering the instrument useless to you. Use the CDV-700 if no reading is obtained by the CDV-715. The CDV-700 has come under criticism for range limitation, reliability, and calibration requirements. Also, headphones are necessary for the CDV-700 in order for the user to be efficient. I have a CDV-715. The government is upgrading to the CDV-718, a digital instrument that signals newer survey instruments are the future. A surplus CDV-715 is available today for less than $100 on the internet. Should you want an updated new state-of-the-art super-duper model then try the Sargent-Welch model CP71252-02 for $718.

The U.S. Customs Service is moving to belt-type beepers that will "chirp" should radiation be encountered. These beepers may be the way to go for size, portability, ease and convenience. The model I purchased is the NuKAlert Personal Radiation Monitor for about $100. The product comes with a scale to allow the user to know how much radiation is present by the number of "chirps." A scale is conveniently located on the back of the device along with a separate scale to indicate how long it would be before the user received 100 roentgens. The NuKAlert will measure as low as 0.1R/Hr. and up to 50R/Hr+. The monitor works 24/7, seven days a week, on a ten-year lithium battery. Russell Manufacturing also has a digital alarm that displays the actual dose rate and is worn on the belt. The brand name is <u>Radalarm</u> and sells for $250-$280.

The equipment you choose will assist in determining the amount of radiation present. Whether your monitor is chattering or chirping only indicates you are being exposed in a radioactive contaminated field. The equipment will not tell you what direction you must take for evacuation or the wind direction the wind nor does the equipment indicate how much or what kind of shielding is required. The monitors are telling you to take defensive action and to take it now not later.

INDIVIDUAL EXTERNAL DOSIMETRY

A dosimeter is used to monitor an individual to determine the total radiation dose received. A dosimeter keeps track of the radiation received. A recharging or change of dosimeters is required so a user must keep a log of the dose received and add the totals to know what level of exposure has been acquired. There are three major dosimeter types in use. They are the pocket ionization chambers, thermo-luminescent dosimeters, and film dosimeters. A combination of these three may also be used since each type has deficient qualities.

A pocket ionization chamber primarily measures whole body gamma exposure. The advantage to this chamber is that the user can read it at any time and total a cumulative exposure dose. They are known to be accurate and easy to recharge with no maintenance required. They are however sensitive to damage if dropped and their cost is high. The main downside is ionization detectors can only detect gamma radiation. It can be worn like a pen in your pocket or clipped to a belt. You can set one outside for an hour to obtain a current radiation rate. Finally, you don't need a radiation survey meter if you have a dosimeter and are not in a hurry. I'll probably be in a big hurry so I prefer my old fashioned CDV-715 survey meter. I want that background chattering noise, along with the chirping of my NuKAlert, to notify me to danger.

The most common civil defense pocket ionization dosimeter models on the market are the CDV-742 and CDV-740. The 742 model reads from 0-200 roentgens and the 740 model from 0-100 roentgens. Both are available from Coleman's Surplus (1-888-478-7758) for about $10 each. You will also require a dosimeter charger. Add about $40 for the CDV-750 charger.

A film dosimeter or film badge can read gamma and beta radiation. They are small and inexpensive. The downside is the film can't be read immediately. Other equipment (densitometer) is required to read the film. Heat or humidity can also affect the reading.

A thermo-luminescent dosimeter (TLD) can read gamma, beta, and neutron exposure. They can store information for long periods of time, are reusable, and are useful in varying radiation fields. The downside is they can't be analyzed immediately and heat or humidity may affect the reading.

Because of the limiting factors with each type a combination of the three or all three may be used by an individual at the same time. An extra downside to all types is they can be lost or if in an area of contamination the dosimeter itself may become contaminated.

A quantum leap forward in electronic dosimeter technology is available with the MPG DMC 2000 series. The unit has a top mounted LCD display and can give you the current dose rate and/or the accumulated dose. It eliminates the need to keep a log. The price is just over $300. While the price is much higher than the other models it also eliminates the possibility of human error to a great degree and keeps your equipment needs to a minimum. A belt holder is available, Order online from geodatasys.com (1-440-888-4749).

BODY DEFENSE

There are four major pathways for radioactive nuclides to enter the body. There is inhalation, ingestion, absorption, and breaks in the skin.

Should you be standing outside in the path of a smoke plume from an accidental plant discharge it is likely radioactive particles will be inhaled. Should you walk unprotected through a field covered with fallout dust it is likely radioactive particles will be inhaled. The defense is to get inside to protection and/or wear a mask. What kind of mask you ask? A common surgical operating room mask will have to do if a proper respirator mask is not available. The mask is specifically the N-95 designated mask. While not designated nor approved as a specific radiological mask it is effective on 0.3 micron sized particles. The problem is a correct fit cannot be obtained with this mask. So contaminants can enter around the edge of the mask where it meets your face. The use of a handkerchief, scarf, or painter's mask will not suffice. You can buy a carton of N-95 for about $40 but it would be much wiser to buy an upgrade to a respirator mask. I only have on hand the N-95 but I know the mask is insufficient.

Respirator masks that have a secure fit, with no leakage where dust can enter are most recommended. 3M Company manufactures a full-face respirator for just over $100 and an additional

$7 for a pair of filters. While this appears to be one of the most popular models we have to keep in mind the 80,000 plus coal miners suing 3M and other manufacturers contending the manufacturers made claims concerning the effectiveness or ease of use of their respirator mask. Basically the plaintiff's attorney said, "You have more and more of these guys wearing respirators who are getting the disease (silicosis, pneumoconiosis, or black lung) at the same rate as the old guys,"[6] that didn't use respirators.

Since the suit includes the major manufacturers that make and market the best safety equipment in the world perhaps we need to remember these masks come with adjustable head straps and you must "fit the mask to your face" for the mask to be effective. Should you not "fit the mask" then indeed radioactive nuclides or even coal dust particles will penetrate your defense. The equipment is only as good as the user. However, we also need to realize and remember that wearing a properly fitted mask for long periods of time or all day long is a very physical and mentally taxing effort and apparently even the coal mining unions were not forewarned.

It has been legally established that disposable respirators had a fundamental shortcoming. The U.S. Court of Appeals in a decision co-written by future Supreme Court Justice Ruth Bader Ginsburg, agreed with OHSA

---

[6] The Courier Journal, Louisville, KY, December 13, 2003

that there was no test for daily use to adequately ensure "the proper fit for disposable respirators."[7] If you can't check fit then you can't be assured of protection. In the world of respirators that's a cardinal rule. Also, the user must make frequent checks to ensure the fit is still correct.

I served as officer-in-charge of gas chamber training exercises for a few years in the military. There were many instances of soldiers with tearful and burning eyes from the CS gas entering a protective mask. However, there was never an instance of equipment failure. Every instance was due to user failure to properly fit the mask. Do remember though, every filter has a shelf life whether used or not and also every filter eventually becomes overloaded with contaminants. Should your filter reach its age or limit then the filter will no longer be effective.

To ensure your mask fits, if a military model, slide the mask over your head, adjust the holding straps, and cover the filter parts with your hand so that air may not pass through. Inhale deeply and if the mask is a fit then the side of the mask will partially collapse inward from the negative pressure. You will be able to feel this happen or see this occurrence on someone else testing for proper fit. If there is no collapsing noted or air is heard or noted entering the sides of the mask then you do not have a fit. Readjust your head straps and try again. Try as many times as is

---

[7] U.S. News & World Report, August 9, 2004, P.41

necessary to get it right. It would be wise to have the fit completed and the mask ready should it ever be needed.

The ultimate defense for inhalation is to be trained and personally fitted for your choice of self-contained breathing apparatus (SCBA). [8] These are the mask types you see firemen wearing. A fireman needs to keep protected from smoke or end up in respiratory deep trouble. This is the same principle as keeping out radioactive particles. There are many of these products available dependent upon your price range and required accessories. Look for a model approved by the National Institute for Occupational Safety and Health. Respirators certified will be labeled "NIOSH Approved" and the label will specify the hazards for which the respirator is approved. Training is required with every model. A training manual is provided by the manufacturer on every NIOSH approved SCBA. On-line training programs are available for a reasonable fee.

The ideal ingestion defense is to eat only canned food and drink only bottled water. Should you pluck an apple from a tree located in an area contaminated with fallout it is possible to ingest nuclides if not properly cleansed. Even then a risk remains. Should you consume a fish caught in contaminated waters then it is likely you will ingest radioactive particles.

---

[8] FEMA, Radiological Emergency Response Independent Study Course, IS 301, January 1998, P.3-29

Should your bare skin be exposed it is possible for some radioactive nuclides to be absorbed. Should you stand under fallout material then it is likely falling beta particles will be absorbed. The eye can be an entry point. The defense is to cover as much skin as possible wearing long sleeves, gloves, and cap where appropriate. Cover your eyes with goggles.

Exposed tissue, such as a wound, may serve as a portal of entry for contamination. The defense is to dress the wound as soon as possible with uncontaminated material.

A room air-cleaner with a High Efficiency Particulate Arrestor (HEPA) filter should be used in the room in which you take shelter if electricity is available to power the machine. HEPA was developed during WWII by the Atomic Energy Commission to remove and capture radioactive dust particles from the air that might present a health hazard. HEPA filters are effective down to 0.3 micron-size particles that pass easily into the body's respiratory systems. 1 micron equals 1 millionth of a meter. A particle that is in size ten microns or less is not visible to the naked eye. For a filter to be labeled "true HEPA" it must be certified 99.97% efficient in capturing 0.3 micron-size particles. A filter labeled as HEPA-Type is not a HEPA filter. A "true HEPA" filter and appropriate size room air-cleaner would go a long way toward reducing air contamination in your shelter.

Reducing the probability of contamination by radioactive particles is our prime motive in all our actions to better insure our survivability. The objective is **ALARA** the acronym for **as low as reasonably achievable**. Remember this acronym and use as your rallying cry whether sheltering or evacuating. The term can become a functional and motivational term for any group of hardy survivors and help them to keep their goal in mind. **ALARA! ALARA! ALARA!** But not too loud or with your mouth open because you don't want to inhale or ingest any lurking contaminated particles. It might be best to write the acronym on a piece of paper and then hold it up in plain sight every once in awhile as a reminder.

Keeping **ALARA** in mind, an article in the *London Telegraph* describes a grim but fascinating view of the quarter-century-old aftermath of the disaster. After signing a waiver, visitors are driven at "breakneck speed, and told not to touch any of the irradiated vegetation or metal structures," writes the *Telegraph*'s Andrew Osborn (A day-long tour package costs about $160) Osborne quotes a guide as saying: "Let's leave now. It is very dangerous to be here."[9] These folk definitely are not educated in how to survive radioactivity!

You may encounter the acronym REM, as I previously mentioned earlier, for Roentgen Equivalent Man. Generally speaking, roentgen, RAD, and REM can be considered roughly equal

---

[9] USA Today reprint posted March 25, 2011, Jayne Clark

although REM is used to account for biological damage. RAD (Radiation Absorbed Dose) is the acronym used to describe the energy absorbed when exposed to a nuclide such as radioactive iodine or plutonium. Thus, while radioactive iodine will cause thyroid cancer we also know that just one particle of radioactive plutonium will cause lung cancer because the nuclide puts out more energy and destroys tissue at a faster rate (perhaps twenty times faster) than other particles. Therefore, the radioactive plutonium will have a greater REM than radioactive iodine that may take multiple nuclides to permanently cause thyroid cancer at a later date. Radioactive iodine will, however, destroy thyroid tissue much faster than plutonium. Think of REM as having a multiplier effect. REM measurement is analogous to choosing the quickest acting poison on any given tissue. At any rate, we do not have the instrumentation available for you to measure your REM dose. There are whole body counters. They are very expensive and it is doubtful one would even be made available at an evacuation shelter. The important note to remember is whatever RAD you have accumulated is going to remain with you and the total dose will more than likely determine your chance of survival. **ALARA!**

EVACUATING

There is a 50-mile radius considered for evacuation around every commercial nuclear power plant in the country. The planning is for an accidental radioactive plume escaping from the power plant. Thus, we can assume we need to get a minimum of 50-miles away should we hear of an accident. Listen to you radio or television stations to know what direction to head since roads may be closed to debris, damage, contamination, or exposed power lines.

I live 120 miles north of Knoxville directly in the path of the usual prevailing wind direction. I would expect fallout to arrive in just over two hours if the wind is blowing at 50 MPH. I need to evacuate and go west to avoid the fallout. If I lived south of Knoxville and the wind generally blows in a northerly direction perhaps I might not evacuate. After all, the contaminants are not being dispersed to my area. Watch your local meteorological report on a regular basis to know the usual origins of wind direction and the Doppler to obtain the usual arrival time of incoming weather to know the usual speed.

Stores including those for food, clothing, and other necessary items will probably be closed. Medical clinics and hospitals will be overwhelmed with demand for their services. The phone lines will be swamped with people seeking information.

State and local police along with the National Guard are designated to direct and monitor traffic. Evacuation remains a thorny issue since the 06' Hurricanes Katrina and Rita and now the 2011 Fukushima Dai-Ichi disaster. Following the Katrina debacle, officials in Texas decided to open all interstate lanes to outbound traffic in Houston with Hurricane Rita bearing down and still suffered a 15-hour traffic logjam. Hurricanes Katrina and Rita provided the evidence requiring further study and change in disaster evacuation scenarios.

Any travel through a contaminated area will result in contamination to your vehicle. Tires are the most dangerous culprit. The rubber will retain most or much of the contamination acquired from fallout on the highways. Therefore, the tires should be changed every 50 to 75-miles when exposed to contamination. Make sure you have cash with which to purchase new or even recaps if changing tires often. Duct tape for the car windows may be very helpful. Do not use the vehicle air conditioner. The rest of the vehicle can be washed with an uncontaminated soap and water source to remove fallout. However, some parts of the vehicle will remain radioactive due to absorption of contaminants. Also, if you use a car wash, the water is recycled and may already be contaminated and useless. You really need or have access to a survey instrument to know whether to keep or dispose of the vehicle. At any rate, you should take the opportunity to decontaminate yourself when you decontaminate the vehicle. I don't think anybody will be cited for public nudity and if so the citation will probably be the least of your problems.

Hair clippers are a valuable tool. This is because **hair** will retain radioactivity much more than other external body parts. So, in dealing with radioactivity let us resolve to shave off all exterior hair. Normally this would just be the head but if other body parts have been bared to contaminants then off with that hair also. Should you unknowingly bathe in contaminated water then removal of all body hair is required for safety. Again, if you have no survey instrument available then proceed on the assumption the water is radioactively contaminated. Remember though, **eyebrows** and possibly lashes will not grow back if shaved off so only trim carefully. Please do not use cosmetic eyelashes or eyebrow liner during the crises.

Evacuation in this country probably means you will be directed to a shelter operated by the Red Cross, Salvation Army, or other charitable groups.

Whatever paper cash you carry with you make sure it is covered or enclosed in a container to avoid contamination. Jewelry, gold or silver coins hoarded for emergency use should be in a metal lined container or otherwise these coins and jewelry may become irradiated and disposal becomes necessary. The same goes for loose change. Please do not wear jewelry in a radioactive time of crises.

Hopefully water is available in bottled form for the trip. If not, drain some water from the building pipes or scoop out water from the toilet tank, not the toilet, into uncontaminated containers.

Pets are not welcome or allowed in any evacuation site you are directed. Another facility will have to be located should you decide to provide for "Rover" or "Kitty." Some guides advise to make a provision for leaving the pet behind with someone you know. Yah-sure! If you're leaving what makes you think someone is going to stay behind and watch your pet? Another source advises that one possibility is to board the pet with a veterinary service once you reach an uncontaminated area. I'm sure the pet will have to be uncontaminated to be accepted. Any positive reading for radiation will probably result in the veterinarian rejecting your pet. Remember the problem with hair? It's going to be real difficult to shave contaminated hair off of a pet. This is a vexing problem and there is no easy solution here. The Russians shot all strays after the Chernobyl meltdown. Your contaminated pet may need to be disposed in a humane manner to protect you and your family. **ALARA**!

Large animals such as cows and horses will have to be evacuated with you to avoid contamination. Hopefully, you will have the necessary trucks and trailers. Otherwise put out as much available food and water and remember these animals will probably become contaminated and need to be destroyed. Again, the Russians solved the problem by destroying the animals. We need to plan ahead for an accident or terrorist strike since we are all vulnerable to radiation. When the unexpected does happen, routines change drastically, and people are suddenly aware of how fragile their lives can be.[10] Hopefully, you made prearranged plans with your family to call "Uncle Bob or Aunt Bee" or some other relative in order to keep in contact with each other and make plans to relocate if necessary. Other measures used to keep in contact with your family include leaving a notice in your front yard or on the door. The Red Cross and FEMA also maintain electronic websites to locate missing family. A cell phone for every family member may be the technology that becomes the solution to maintaining contact. However, a cell phone may not be operable if there has been a nuclear explosion. The Electro-Magnetic Pulse (EMP) Commission reported the wireless system is technologically fragile in relation to EMP. In general, wireless may be so seriously degraded in the EMP region as to be unavailable. If cell phone service is unavailable due to jamming and you have text availability communication may work because text messaging requires less data than voice transmission. Reports coming from Japan verified this theory but no EMP was present. What

---

[10] P. 5.1 A Citizen's Guide to Disaster Assistance, IS-7, Emergency Management Institute, FEMA, Sep. 2003

kind of government assistance can we expect once we evacuate to a shelter? The president must declare a disaster before federal assistance can begin. Most federal assistance is in the form of low-interest loans. So you will basically be starting your financial life over again. At least the loans will enable you and the community to escape dire poverty while rebuilding your life.

Should you not be able to qualify for a federal loan then you can request housing assistance that can include the following: lodging expense reimbursement for a hotel or motel, rental assistance in the form of a cash payment for a temporary rental unit or manufactured unit, home repair or replacement cash grant, or permanent housing construction in rare circumstances. Other needs covered include medical, dental, funeral, transportation and other disaster related needs. The maximum coverage per individual or household assistance is $26,200. That probably won't go far.

FEMA officials will be available near or at shelters to assist you with your claims (you must present identification) or you can call their help-line at 1-800-621-FEMA (3362). Depending on your insurance and other resources there may be a program to help you.

FUTURE MEDICAL TREATMENTS

Hollis-Eden Pharmaceuticals is researching the effects of radiation on primates and is developing a new drug named NEUMONE (HE 2100). The drug will be used to prevent bone marrow suppression from acute radiation injury. Protection may be provided for exposure up to 400 RAD. The company is also working on the development of PHOSPHONOL to prevent DNA mutations from radiation exposure.[11]

---

[11] P. 16-19, Hollis Eden Pharmaceuticals 2003 Annual Report

TEST

The following questions will cover most of the material in the book. Once every member of the family has read the material treat the questions in the framework of *Jeopardy* or *Trivia* whether sheltering, evacuating, or planning. The goal is not to score 70% or 90%, but to score 100% and understand the answer and substantive knowledge behind each. The reason for the goal is to increase an individual or family's survivability chances.

1. The one announcement we hope to never hear in a time of crises;
    A. Play ball
    B. Gentlemen, start your engines
    C. This is not a test
    D. Choose heads or tails

2. The first indication of a nuclear blast is
    A. Sonic boom
    B. Bright white or yellow flash
    C. Distant thunder
    D. Smoke filled sky

3. The Flash-to-Bang time Rule of Thumb estimates
   A. Time
   B. Damage
   C. Kiloton or megaton rating
   D. Range

4. We observe the flash of a nuclear explosion and hear the bang in two minutes and thirty seconds later. The approximate range is
   A. 3 miles
   B. 13 miles
   C. 23 miles
   D. 33 miles

5. The greatest threat from a nuclear explosion in addition to radiation is
   A. Airborne objects capable of striking damage
   B. Building collapse
   C. Sunburn
   D. Airborne bacteria

6. What is the best first reaction on glimpsing a nuclear flash?
   A. Run home to your basement
   B. Wait for further directions
   C. Take cover in a ditch five yards away
   D. Drop flat onto a neighbor's lawn

7.	Leave your first line of defense
	A.	Once the blast wave has passed
	B.	Once a reverse blast wave is noted
	C.	When a passing neighbor offers you a ride home
	D.	After the "All Clear" announcement

8.	The construction material best suited for defense and epitomized by the story of "The Three Little Pigs" is
	A.	Brick
	B.	Straw
	C.	Wood
	D.	Stucco

9.	The four types of radiation
	A.	Neutral, Charlie, Delta, X-ray
	B.	Gamma, Beta, Alpha, Neutron
	C.	Phi Gamma Jamma
	D.	Neutral, Positive, Atomic, Hydrogen

10.	Generally, the first type of radiation you may be exposed
	A.	Microwave
	B.	Computer
	C.	Toaster
	D.	Gamma

11.	The type of radiation that does not cause continuous exposure
	A.	Neutron

B. Alpha
C. Beta
D. Gamma

12. Once received a radiation dose is
     A. Good for 24 hours
     B. An x-ray
     C. Irreversible
     D. Provided on a continuous basis

13. A mushroom cloud carries
     A. Radioactive contaminants
     B. Rain
     C. Vitamins
     D. Immunization

14. The first nuclide to defend against is
     A. Cesium
     B. Iodine
     C. Strontium
     D. Plutonium

15. Thyroid cancer is caused by a nuclide of
     A. Plutonium
     B. Strontium
     C. Iodine
     D. Cesium

16. The best defense against thyroid cancer if
     exposure is expected
     A. Potassium iodide tablets

B. Sodium chloride tablets

C. KI

D. Both A and C

17. The usual adult dose of potassium chloride

A. Taken for 2 days only

B. Wait for government instructions

C. 130 mg tablet

D. Both A and C

18. Protection from other nuclides is provided by

A. None

B. Vitamins

C. Apples

D. Oranges

19. KI is legally available

A. Over-the-counter

B. Online

C. Only with a prescription

D. Both A and B

20. The government plan for dissemination of KI is

A. Probably too time consuming

B. In conjunction with the postal service

C. Probably inadequate

D. All of the above

21. Do not ingest KI if you are allergic to

A. Shellfish or iodine
B. Swordfish or iodine
C. Swordfish or mushrooms
D. Shellfish or mushrooms

22. Surviving nuclear radiation is dependent upon
A. Age, sex, religion
B. Age, health, antibiotics
C. Age, health, religion
D. Time, distance, shielding

23. The best shielding is provided by
A. Lead, wood
B. Concrete, wood
C. Lead, iron
D. Tinting, wood

24. If the outside reading is 1400R/Hr then the expected outside dose in 21 hours using the 7:10 rule of thumb is
A. 14R/Hr
B. 21R/Hr
C. 140R/Hr
D. 210R/hr

25. If the outside dose rate is calculated to 30R/Day the expected outside dose rate in one week is
A. 60R/Day
B. 3R/Day

C. 30R/Day

D. 210R/Day

26. The best source of radioactive readings are available from
    A. Television
    B. Radio
    C. Newspaper
    D. A personal digital survey meter

27. A dirty bomb is
    A. A nuclear explosion measured in kiloton
    B. A mushroom cloud carrying dirt
    C. Contaminated with dirt
    D. Standard explosive device spreading shards of nuclide products

28. If you live in Manhattan and a dirty bomb is detonated
    A. Join the bottle-necked bumper-to-bumper traffic evacuating the city
    B. Go to your apartment and stay inside
    C. Close all windows and seal any openings
    D. B and C

29. If you live in Manhattan and hear a dirty bomb detonation occurred on Staten Island
    A. Go home and shut all windows
    B. Shower to remove contaminants
    C. Listen to the news for further advice
    D. All of the above

30. The radiation from a chest x-ray is
    A. Alpha
    B. Beta
    C. Neutrino
    D. Gamma

31. The chest x-ray _____ you from/to radiation
    A. Blistered
    B. Exempted
    C. Exposes
    D. Contaminates

32. Structural cell damage may be caused by
    A. Gamma
    B. Alpha
    C. Beta
    D. All of the above

33. Radioactive exposure occurs by
    A. Ingestion of nuclides
    B. Eating the nuclides
    C. Inhaling the nuclides
    D. All of the above

34. The radioactive half-life of a nuclide is
    measured
    A. Age of victim
    B. Time
    C. If the nuclide is divided
    D. Gallons

35. A dairy farmer owns 30 milk cows that are grain fed from a metal container located in the barn. Unknown to the farmer, heavy fallout contaminates his pasture land. The farmer milks the cows with automatic equipment and stores the milk in stainless steel containers. Is the milk safe to drink?

    A. Probably, unless the farmer's footwear contaminates the milking site from nuclides stirred up by the trudge from farmhouse to barn
    B. Probably, but remember the milk is not pasteurized.
    C. None of the above
    D. A and B

36. Consider all living animals within a fallout area

    A. Contaminated
    B. As a food source
    C. Fair game
    D. None of the above

37. The safest source of meat in a fallout area

    A. Fish
    B. MRE's
    C. Canned
    D. B and C

38. The safest eggs to eat in a fallout zone

A. Fresh and well cooked
B. Raw eggs
C. Broken eggs
D. None of the above

39. Vegetables in the garden not harvested
A. Will be contaminated
B. Require cleaning with safe water
C. Require peeling
D. All of the above

40. Fruit not harvested
A. Will require cleaning with safe water
B. Will be contaminated
C. Require peeling
D. All of the above

41. The best source of food
A. Is planted and eaten fresh by you
B. Is from hunting
C. Is canned   i
D. Is from fishing

42. The liquid in canned green beans
A. Should be drained due to preservatives
B. Used for hydration
C. Must be boiled
D. Is contaminated

43. The best source of uncontaminated water
A. Prefilled jugs of water

B. Boiled water
C. The closest lake habituated by water fowl
D. Rain water

44. Other sources to obtain water prior to fallout
A. B, C, and D
B. Water in a toilet tank reservoir
C. Bathtub filled with water from the dwelling's main line
D. Sink filled with water from the dwelling's main line

45. A nuclear tan is
A. Obtained in Mexico
B. Caused by 100 RADs or more
C. The reason nuclear plant workers never frolic on the beach
D. Offered by tanning salons

46. A prominent sign of a nuclear tan is
A. Rotting teeth
B. Applied cosmetics
C. Powdery looking face
D. Flaking skin

47. Radiation poisoning indicates
A. Some part of the body has been affected
B. Structural cell damage

C. A and B
D. None of the above

48. A fetus can tolerate ___ RADs without inflicting genetic disorders
A. 10
B. 5
C. 100
D. 0

49. A pregnant woman should not be exposed to radiation levels above
A. A 10 RADs
B. 5 RADs
C. 100 RADs
D. 0 RADs

50. A lethal dose of radiation is ___ RADs and above
A. 300
B. 600
C. 450
D. 100

51. No deaths are expected in a group receiving up to ___ RADs
A. 200
B. 1000
C. 2000
D. 4000

52. The best shielding is provided by
    A. Ice, wood, snow, steel
    B. Wood, snow, steel, brick
    C. Snow, steel, brick, concrete
    D. Iron, steel, brick, concrete

53. The best shielding is measured in
    A. Half-value layer thickness
    B. Half-life
    C. 7:10 Rule of Thumb
    D. Flash-to-Bang Time

54. The "tenth value" thickness of concrete is eleven inches. A box type structure covered on all sides by twenty-two inches of concrete with an outside reading of 100R/Hr should have an inside reading of
    A. 1R/hr
    B. 10R/hr
    C. 100R/hr
    D. None of the above

55. Who maintains a log to reunite families
    A. State National Guard
    B. State police
    C. Red Cross
    D. Most local electric companies

56. Radio reports indicate 55R/Hr fallout. The best survey instrument is
    A. CDV-715

B. CDV-700
C. CDV-718
D. CDV-715 with headphones

57. The preferred individual dosimeter is the
A. MPG 2000 Series
B. CDV-740
C. CDV-742
D. CDV-750

58. You see a radioactive plume heading in your direction. Sufficient protection includes
A. An umbrella
B. A rain coat
C. A Halloween mask
D. None of the above

59. The advantage of the MPG DMC 2000 Series
A. Eliminates the need to keep a log
B. Reduces the possibility of human error
C. Keeps equipment needs to a minimum
D. All of the above
E. None of the above
F. A and C only

60. A cardinal rule of respirators
A. If you can't check fit, you can't be assured of protection
B. Is a single use design
C. The equipment must be better than the user

D. A and C

E. None of the above

61. The ultimate defense for inhalation is to be trained and personally fitted for your choice of
A. SCBA
B. SPCA
C. N-95
D. Halloween mask

62. Certified respirators contain a label indicating
A. CR Approved
B. NIOSH Approved
C. SPCA Approved
D. For Professional Use Only

63. A room air cleaner with ___ filter may be used in your shelter if electricity is available
A. HEPA Type
B. Disposable
C. HEPA
D. Washable
E. None of the above

64. ___ may be used as a warning acronym during a radioactive emergency
A. ALARA, ALARA, ALARA
B. Geronimo, Geronimo, Geronimo
C. Tora, Tora, Tora

D. Good eye, good eye, good eye

65.   Reducing the amount of radiation received
       is our prime motive to insure our
       survivability and is done by
       A. Propagating the human race
       B. Defeating the enemy
       C. Dose received is as low as reasonably
           achievable
       D. A and C
       E. None of the above

66.   What part of the vehicle may be most
       contaminated during evacuation?
       A. Coolant
       B. Tires
       C. Air conditioner
       D. Headlights

67.   What body part may become most
        contaminated?
       A. Toe nails
       B. Hair
       C. Hands
       D. Mouth

68.   Responsibility for your protection belongs
       with
       A.   Government
       B.   Fire department
       C. Homeland Security

D. You

Answers					
1-C		31-C		61-A	
2-B		32-D		62-B	
3-D		33-D		63-C	
4-D		34-B		64-A	
5-A		35-D		65-C	
6-C		36-A		66-B	
7-B		37-D		67-B	
8-A		38-A		68-D	
9-B		39-D			
10-D		40-D			
11-D		41-C			
12-C		42-B			
13-A		43-A			
14-B		44-A			
15-C		45-B			
16-D		46-C			
17-D		47-C			
18-A		48-D			
19-D		49-D			
20-D		50-B			
21-A		51-A			
22-D		52-D			
23-C		53-A			
24-A		54-A			
25-B		55-C			
26-D		56-C			
27-D		57-A			
28-D		58-D			

29-D		59-D			
30-D		60-A			

The following questions are to stimulate mental survival instincts, understand ethical beliefs, and realize the sense of morality within a family. There are no correct or incorrect answers.

1.

A family member employed by a nearby nuclear plant receives 20,000 RADs from an accident and returns home immediately knowing the facility body scanner indicates the employee is emitting 10,000 R/Hr. Should the employee be welcomed home? Should the employee have gone elsewhere?

2.

The above affected employee dies within the week. How should the remains be handled? Discuss various funeral rites available.

3.

Your neighbor knows you converted the basement to a fallout shelter. You have stocked the shelter with provisions sufficient for your family. Now, fallout is arriving and the neighbor is beating on the door demanding admission. What do you do?

4.

Your life-long best friend lives ten miles away. There is a nuclear incident. He arrives asking to borrow your only radiological survey instrument to measure the dose rate at his home. He promises to bring the instrument right back. What do you do?

AFTERWORD

A nuclear accident caused by a terrorist, design flaw, or other natural disaster appears inadvertently to be part of future human history.

Recalling the acts of Carlos the Jackal---In 1982, a terrorist team cell led by Carlos (The Jackal) attempted to blow up a nuclear reactor in France. Their rocket-powered explosives were not able to penetrate the facilities concrete walls so the attempt failed.[12]

In January, 1982, Carlos began to lay plans for an attack in France. After forming an alliance with a Swiss extremist group, plans were laid to destroy a nuclear plant that was under construction in central France. Shortly before midnight on January 18, a group including Magdelena Kopp fired an RPG-7 rocket launcher across the river Rhone at the outer shell of the reactor but, despite firing five rockets, failed to penetrate the thick concrete causing only minor damages.[13]

---

[12] Hunting the Jackal, P. 223, Billy Waugh, Avon Books, NY, 2004

[13] Carlos the Jackal: Trail of Terror, Chapter 15, One Man's War, Court TV's Crime Library---
www.crimelibrary.com/terrorists_spies/terrorists/Jackal/15.HTML?sect=22

www.ingramcontent.com/pod-product-compliance
Lightning Source LLC
Chambersburg PA
CBHW060651030426
42337CB00017B/2554